Crystalline Structure I

All cartoons are copyright Alexander Matthews 2009.

The rights of Alexander Matthews to be identified as author of this work has been asserted by him in accordance with the Copyright, Designs and Patents Act, 1988.

ISBN 978-0-557-06025-2

alexandercartoons.com

All rights reserved. No part of this publication may be reproduced or transmitted in any form or means, electronic, mechanical or telepathic without prior written permission from the author.

To Zhenia and to Daisy.

"Yeah? Well this warrant says I *can* tickle you until you wet yourself."

In this volume:

1. *The lives of the objects.*
2. *Dealing with death.*
3. *Animals and how boring they are.*
4. *Business masterliness made easy.*
5. *Ignoring the needs of others.*

1. The lives of the objects.

"I'm a stalagmite trapped inside a stalactite's body. Or possibly vice versa."

"Are you going to eat your cutlery?"

21

> This is a place of work, Harris.
> Go home and change.
>
> — *Alexander*

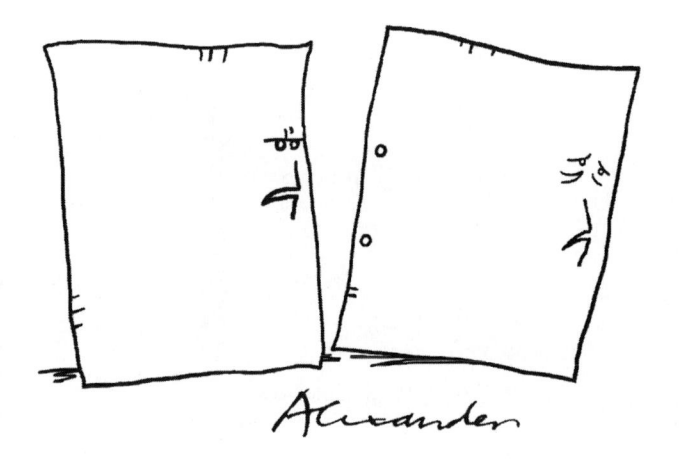

"I've read about a creature that makes marks like these, but I thought it was a myth."

"We're dealing with a real sicko here, Chief."

"Sometimes, Louise, I wonder which one of us is the unfeeling, soulless, monolithic slab."

"I'll twist."

"You're too clingy."

Rock breaks Scissors' heart.

23
Alexander

"Don't get mad, get even!"

"The procedure is very simple. First we carefully remove your skin, then we chop you into tiny pieces before frying you in olive oil."

"It hurts to be called a little piggy, Doc. It really hurts."

"You should have mentioned in your CV that you could only do it once."

"There is excellent opportunity for advancement in this company. I didn't start out as an executive, you know"

"Your scraping is fine, but your bowing needs work."

Clockwise from top left: One, Two, Four, Three.

"You're home early, pumpkin."

"When you say you're a single-celled organism, how do you mean *single*?"

"She's as cute as a button!"

"One of us going to have to eat the other."

"I got dumpt."

"You made the wet patch, you sleep in it."

2. Dealing with death.

"On 3…"

"This next song is about death and how it comes to us all."

"This is such a surprise darling, especially since I buried you under the patio 3 years ago."

"He's still so full of life, although it's mostly larval."

"I'm looking for a tie that says, 'Cower before the architect of your destruction, pathetic earthling fools.'"

"Nothing for me, thanks."

Sadly, close to 90% of these archbishops will be picked off by predators before they ever reach the safety of the ocean.

"Dearly beheaded, we are gathered here today…"

"Stand by to see if his hair sticks to the balloon."

"It's half price because the genie inside it is dead."

"You call that a blaze of glory?"

"It's a long journey, so I thought you could learn to take apart, clean and reassemble this AK47."

"Very nice. What else did you learn at your Hara-Kiri class?"

"Bad day?"

"Did you ever walk into a room to do something, but once you're there you can't for the life of you remember what it was?"

"You can't tell, but the one on the left is a mobile phone mast."

"My last boyfriend had a sex-change, killed me and stole my identity."

"Will that be all, Sir?"

3. Animals and how boring they are.

"Drink plenty of fluids and stay out of the sun."

"In this department we work hard and, if the cat's away, we play hard."

"You're a cruel dog."

"Is everything okay with your meal?"

"I've had it converted into flats."

"He's a shiitake."

"This one I bagged by accident when I was cleaning my harpoon in a paddling pool."

"Get a job!"

"What's that boy? Someone needs my help? Soufflé trouble?"

"He's on holiday."

"I wish I had the guts to go out like that."

"I can't leave, I have an egg balanced on my feet."

"The gentleman at the end of the bar would like to buy you a dead mouse."

"The ball of wool channel? Who the hell signed us up for that?"

"How many more times is it going to circle the planet?"

"The bowl of meat on the floor looks good."

"He's not one of the greats, but he's good for a cat."

"I see you've already met my husband."

"Contrary to our intentions, morale seems to have actually *decreased* since we unleashed the rhino."

"Are you finished with the giant squid section?"

"My, Grandma, what a high definition TV you have."

"Roll over! Not play dead!"

"Why is it that you're always being eaten by a tiger when I call you in here, Popper?"

"I ordered it an hour and a half ago!"

"She wants the hutch and the burrow, but she says you can keep the top hat."

"The reason you have to learn these new tricks, Wilson, is because the old tricks are not compatible with Windows Vista."

"Down boy."

"How did that make you feel, when they flushed your wife down the toilet?"

4. Business masterliness made easy.

"It's a good guess Simmons, but no, I haven't asked you in here for snuggles."

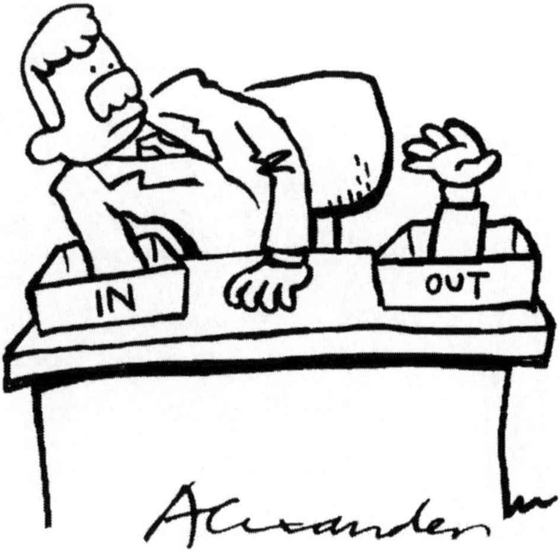
IN
OUT
Alexander

"If you find me an intimidating boss, try picturing me clothed."

"A Mr Stebson and associate, sir. To carry you out in a box."

"Your CV is rather thin."

"It's about the english mahogony 72 inch classic executive desk."

"I've taken the liberty of telling my dying mother that I already got the job."

"Miss Jones, get me another eyebrow."

"What a delightful family. Give them to me at once."

"Jean, bring me everything we've got on gravity."

"Human flesh consumption is up 200%. Well done, Wilkins."

"Didn't you get the memo? Dress down friday has been replaced with crystalline structure friday."

"When I read your report, Haskins, I must confess that I stopped hovering for a moment."

"Well so it is! I hadn't noticed that you'd written your CV on a baby."

"Let's make this meeting brief."

"My kids."

"Sandra, can you step in here a minute and lie on the floor? And bring a ramp."

"We're replacing you with a machine."

"Can you start immediately?"

"Impressive, but wheelies will only get you so far in this company, Hodgson."

"This meeting is not for discussing how to deal with the meteorite. It's to draw up a list of possible candidates to review the need to deal with the meteorite."

"You want to take the next *how many* days off?"

5. *Ignoring the needs of others.*

"I think we've made a real breakthrough today."

"Mum, Dad, this is the haircut I'm going to spend the rest of my life with."

"This is a well organised, if somewhat confusing protest."

"These nappies are maybe a little *too* absorbant."

"Stop trying to change me."

"You promised me you'd be dressed and ready to go by 8.30, Diane."

"My first wife was not what you'd call a looker."

"Does this invisibility cloak make me look fat?"

"Oh, so now you've turned the furniture against me as well?"

"I was expecting fireworks."

"The last time he came out to play with you, you reassigned his gender."

"Red or white?"

"Perhaps *this* will refresh your memory."

"I think it could have been more faithful to the synopsis of the book I read on Wikipedia."

"Did you have to usurp me in front of everybody?"

"Absent friends."

Setting the table for that special dinner

Right

Wrong

"He'd be perfect for you."

"Love the no taste."

"You got until sundown to think me up a bedtime story, pardner."

"Is it locally sourced?"

"And is there a Mrs Tambourine-Man?"

"Good afternoon, Madam. Have you ever thought about developing an unsightly hump?"

"It's part of life's rich tapestry."